G!ANT BEAVERS

ASHLEY GISH

ICE AGE CREATURES X BOOKS

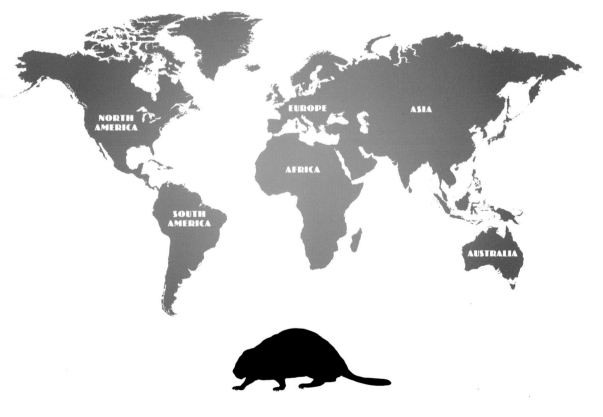

NORTH AMERICA

EUROPE

ASIA

AFRICA

SOUTH AMERICA

AUSTRALIA

CREATIVE EDUCATION · CREATIVE PAPERBACKS

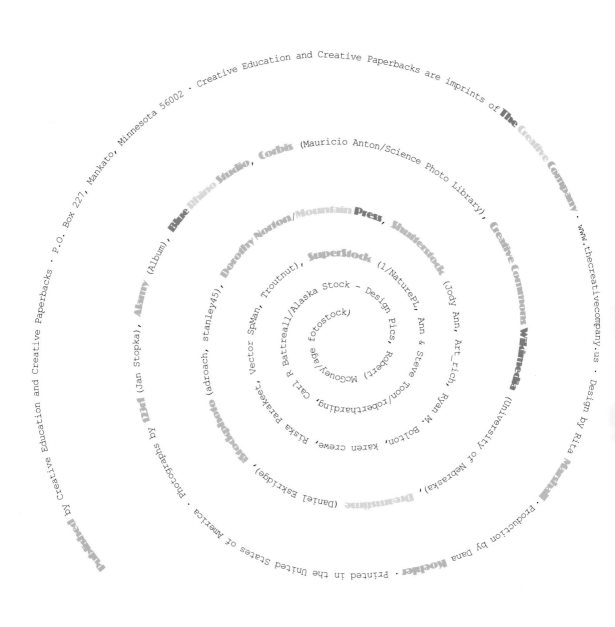

Published by Creative Education and Creative Paperbacks · P.O. Box 227, Mankato, Minnesota 56002 · Creative Education and Creative Paperbacks are imprints of The Creative Company · www.thecreativecompany.us · Design by Rita Marshall · Production by Dana Kessler · Printed in the United States of America · Photographs by Alamy (Jan Stopka), iStock (adroach, stanley45), Blue Rhino Studio, Corbis (Mauricio Anton/Science Photo Library), Dorothy Norton/Mountain Press, Shutterstock (Jody Ann, Art_rich, Ryan M. Bolton, Karen Crewe, Riska parakeet, Vector SpMan, Troutnut), SuperStock (1/NaturePL, Ann & Steve Toon/robertharding, Carl R Battreall/Alaska Stock – Design Pics, Robert McGoueY/age fotostock), Dreamtime (Daniel Eskridge), Getty Images (University of Nebraska)

Library of Congress Cataloging-in-Publication Data • Names: Gish, Ashley, author. • Title: Giant beavers / by Ashley Gish. • Description: Mankato, Minnesota: The Creative Company, [2023] • Series: X-books: ice age creatures • Includes bibliographical references and index. • Audience: Ages 6–8 | Grades 2–3 • Summary: "A countdown of five of the most captivating giant beaver fossil discoveries and relatives provides thrills as readers discover more about the biological, social, and hunting characteristics of these Ice Age creatures" —Provided by publisher. • Identifiers: LCCN 2021044426 | ISBN 9781640264342 (library binding) | ISBN 9781628329674 (paperback) | ISBN 9781640006089 (ebook) • Subjects: LCSH: Beavers, Fossil—Juvenile literature. • Classification: LCC QE882.R6 G57 2023 • DDC 569/.37—dc23/eng/20211116
LC record available at https://lccn.loc.gov/2021044426

GIANT BEAVERS

CONTENTS

ICE AGE CREATURES
X
BOOKS

XCEPTIONAL ANCIENT ANIMALS

During the Ice Age, giant beavers roamed North America. They were as long as an alligator. They weighed as much as a black bear. They had long front teeth. They looked fearsome. But giant beavers ate plants.

Giant Beaver Basics

Giant beavers were large **rodents**. They looked like huge versions of modern beavers. Water rolled right off their oily brown fur. Giant beavers were good swimmers. They used their tail for steering while swimming underwater. They had large **webbed** feet. Huge hind feet made it hard for giant beavers to walk on land.

GIANT BEAVER RANGE

NORTH AMERICA

GIANT BEAVERS roamed North America during the Ice Age.

AMERICAN BEAVER

GIANT BEAVER

Giant beavers were North America's biggest rodents during the Ice Age. Some weighed more than 200 pounds (90.7 kg). They were about eight feet (2.4 m) long from head to tail. Their modern relatives include rats, mice, porcupines, squirrels, and beavers.

Many swamps dried up at the end of the Ice Age.

Giant beavers and modern beavers are both rodents. But they are not closely related.

GIANT BEAVER TOOTH

Giant beavers looked like modern beavers. They behaved like other modern rodents. Their front teeth were six inches (15.2 cm) long. The tips of these teeth were rounded. The back teeth were used for grinding up tough roots, stems, and leaves. Giant beavers ate **aquatic** plants. This diet is similar to muskrats' diets. Giant beavers lived in swamps and ponds on the cold landscape. They died out about 10,000 years ago.

Giant beaver tails were not flat.

ROUNDED TAILS

Giant beavers lived alongside modern beavers for thousands of years.

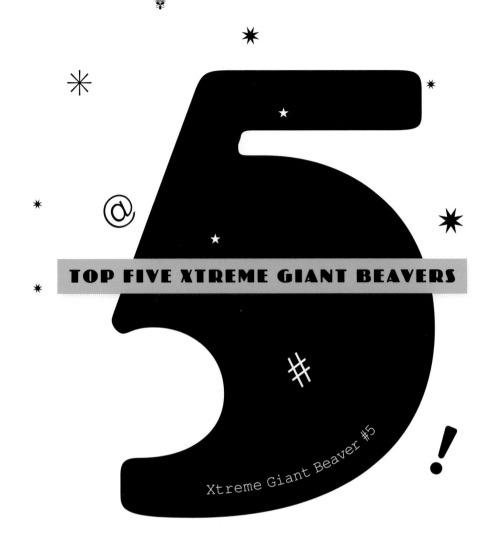

Xtreme Giant Beaver #5

Eurasian Giant *Trogontherium* was a type of giant beaver in Europe. It lived from about 2.5 million years ago until about 10,000 years ago. It ranged from France to China. Researchers think Siberia and northern China were warmer then. This giant beaver lived in swamps. It ate floating plants. Some scientists believe cooling temperatures caused these beavers to die out. Other research suggests Ice Age humans hunted all of these giant beavers.

Giant Beaver Beginnings

An ice age is a period of time when Earth's temperatures fall. Sheets of ice cover the land. Earth has been through at least five ice ages. We call the most recent one the Ice Age. During that time, many animals had to **adapt**. They needed to change to live in colder temperatures. Some animals grew bigger. Their fur became thicker.

Giant beavers thrived in cold places. They shared the land with other large animals. These included bison, mammoths, saber-toothed cats, and dire wolves. Giant beavers probably did not have enemies in the water. They were big, strong swimmers. But these creatures were clumsy on land. A saber-toothed cat could easily catch a slow-moving giant beaver.

1837

1912

1960s

Castoroides ohioensis, Ohio

giant beaver skull and lodge, Ohio

giant beaver jawbone, Minnesota

1995

Castoroides leiseyorum,
Florida

1998

giant beaver incisor,
New Brunswick, Canada

GIANT BEAVER BEGINNINGS FACT

Some giant beavers lived on the tundra. The tundra is cold all the time. The ground is often frozen solid.

TOP FIVE XTREME GIANT BEAVERS

Xtreme Giant Beaver #4

On-Screen Beavers Beavers look friendly.
That's probably why they have been
featured in many children's stories.
Disney's *Lady and the Tramp* (1955)
presents a charming beaver. He is
tricked into removing Lady's muzzle.
*The Chronicles of Narnia: The Lion,
the Witch, and the Wardrobe* (2005)
introduces Mr. and Mrs. Beaver. They are
kind, talented, and tough. Reilly is a
beaver in *Open Season* (2006). He oversees
dam construction in the park where the
animals live.

XTRAORDINARY LIFESTYLE

Giant beavers shared similarities with modern beavers. But modern beavers had advantages that helped them survive the end of the Ice Age. Giant beavers died out.

Kits are born with a full coat of fur.

BEAVER X BABIES

Giant Beaver Society

Most giant beaver **fossils** have been found in the central and eastern United States. Some have been dug up in northwestern Canada. Others have been found in Florida. Researchers believe giant beavers lived in cold, wet places with long summers. These creatures ate aquatic plants. During the summer, they built up their fat stores. This helped them survive the cold winter.

There were two kinds of giant beavers in North America. *Castoroides leiseyorum* lived in the southeastern U.S. Scientists have found *C. leiseyorum* remains that are more than 1.4 million years old! *Castoroides ohioensis* roamed farther north. None of its remains are more than 130,000 years old. The youngest fossils of this creature were found in Minnesota and New York. They are about 10,200 years old.

The first giant beaver fossil was found in Ohio in 1837.

This is where *Castoroides ohioensis* got its name.

XEMPLARY DISCOVERIES

Modern beavers eat mostly wood. Giant beavers did not eat wood. Scientists know this because they have discovered that what you eat stays with you. Scientists found proof of aquatic plants—not wood—in giant beaver fossils.

In 1995, researchers found a fossilized family of beavers in Europe. There were two adults and eight kits. These beavers were called *Steneofiber*. The fossils showed that these ancient beavers lived in family groups. Modern beaver families also live this way. Giant beavers probably lived in family groups, too.

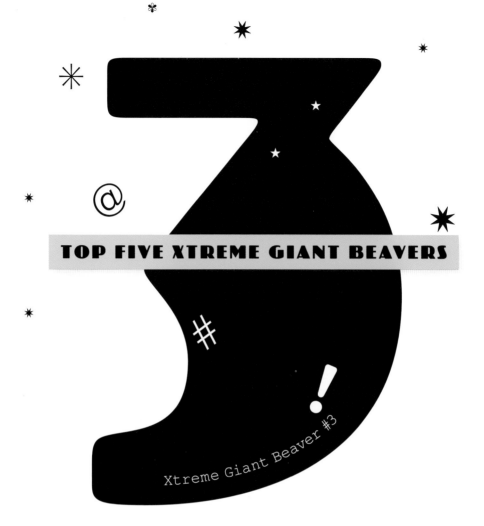

TOP FIVE XTREME GIANT BEAVERS

Xtreme Giant Beaver #3

Close Call Long ago, roughly 400 million Eurasian beavers roamed Europe and Asia. But people hunted them for their fur and oil. By the 1600s, only 1,200 of these beavers were left in the world! Many countries banned people from hunting beavers. Beaver populations rebounded quickly. Now, there are more than 600,000 Eurasian beavers worldwide. They are no longer in danger of dying out.

XASPERATING CONFLICT

Some scientists think rising temperatures might have killed off giant beavers. Others think beavers died from loss of habitat. New research suggests that giant beavers gradually died out.

Giant Beaver Survival

As **glaciers** shrank, giant beavers followed them. They relied on the cool, wet environment of the glaciers. Modern beavers were once hunted for their fur and castoreum. Castoreum is a greasy substance. It is produced at the base of the tail. Beavers use it to leave their scent. It also makes their fur waterproof.

Two kinds of beavers are alive today. These are the American beaver and the Eurasian beaver. They are smaller than their Ice Age relatives. Modern beavers are smart. They build dams and lodges from branches and mud.

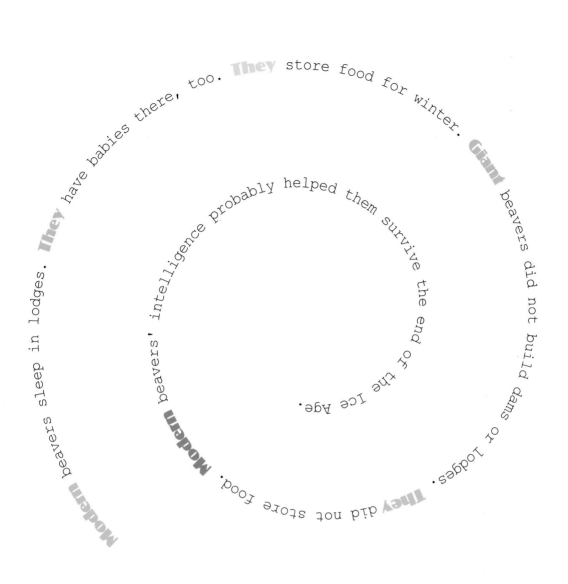

Modern beavers sleep in lodges. They have babies there, too. They store food for winter. Giant beavers did not build dams or lodges. They did not store food. Modern beavers' intelligence probably helped them survive the end of the Ice Age.

GIANT BEAVER SURVIVAL FACT

Modern beavers have flat, chisel-like teeth for gnawing trees. Like giant beavers, their back teeth grind food into a pulp.

Xtreme Giant Beaver #2

Devil's Corkscrews In the mid-1800s, people in Nebraska found strange fossils. They were shaped like corkscrews. People thought they were from ancient plants. They were called "devil's corkscrews." Rodent fossils were found near the corkscrews. Scientists determined that the rodents had made these corkscrews. They were burrows. The tiny rodents, called *Palaeocastor*, were a type of beaver. They died out about 20 million years ago.

Before the Ice Age, beavers dug burrows and lived on land. There were 15 different kinds of these burrowing beavers.

Modern beavers have been around for 10 million years. They originated in Asia and spread across Europe and North America.

The Ice Age began more than a million years ago and ended about 10,000 years ago.

American and Eurasian beavers cannot have babies with each other.

The beavers in the movie *Ice Age: The Meltdown* (2006) are actually based on horned gophers. They lived more than 5 million years ago.

Semiaquatic muskrats are about the same size as rabbits. They live in swampy areas.

The Eurasian beaver is the largest living rodent in Europe and Asia.

Capybaras are also called "water hogs." These large rodents live in South America.

American beavers are slightly smaller than Eurasian beavers. Both animals can weigh 70 pounds (31.8 kg).

Many rodents are active at night and asleep during the day. Giant beavers may have behaved the same way.

Steneofiber were small. They were just 12 inches (30.5 cm) long. Like other beavers, they could waterproof their fur.

Castoroides leiseyorum is also called the Florida beaver. Researchers thought it lived only in Florida.

Giant beavers had a rounded tail. Modern beavers have a flat tail that is used to steer while swimming.

Beaver kits live in their parents' lodge until they

are about two years old. Kits of different ages may live in one lodge.

TOP FIVE XTREME GIANT BEAVERS

Xtreme Giant Beaver #1

Giant Beavers and Ancient Humans Imagine walking among mammoths, ground sloths, and giant beavers. Scientists believe humans lived at the same time as these creatures. Fossilized spear points were discovered near giant beaver fossils at the Sheriden Cave Pit Fossil Site in Ohio. Researchers do not think that the spear points were used to hunt giant beavers. But fossil dating suggests these animals shared the land with humans.

GLOSSARY

adapt – adjust to new conditions

aquatic – growing and living in water

fossils – the remains of once-living things preserved in rock

glaciers – slow-moving masses of ice

habitat – the natural home of plants and animals

rodents – animals that have strong front teeth used for gnawing

webbed – connected by a web of skin

RESOURCES

Patent, Dorothy Hinshaw. *At Home with the Beaver: The Story of a Keystone Species*. Berkeley, Calif.: Web of Life Children's Books, 2019.

Van Brenk, Debora. "A Giant Beaver Tale of Extinction." Western News. https://news.westernu.ca/2019/05/a-giant-beaver-tale-of-extinction/.

Zoehfeld, Kathleen Weidner. *Prehistoric: Dinosaurs, Megalodons, and Other Fascinating Creatures of the Deep Past*. Greenbelt, Md.: What on Earth Books, 2019.

INDEX

People use castoreum in perfume and food. It smells like leather.